*Presented to*

.................................................

*By*

.................................................

*On This Date*

.................................................

# BY THIS
# FIRE

# GLORIA
# GAITHER

## acknowledgments

A special thanks to my sister, evelyn, and her husband, dave, for their help and support in this project and to nancy wood at *expressions photography* for capturing the fire and warmth our family has shared for more than three decades.

# preface

Bill and i still live in the house we built thirty-some years ago when we were both high school english teachers ❧ three children have grown up here ❧ they were cradled and diapered here, celebrated and congratulated here ❧ now four children of the new millennium generation hide in these trees, roll down the hillside, and fish in the same creek their parents did ❧ the newly married school teachers who planned and built this house now answer to "mamaw" and "papaw."

the house has metamorphosed over the years into its present size, shape, and function ❧ the original two-car garage became the first office/shipping room for gaither music company, then matured into a big warm family room ❧ the original family room is now the master bedroom ❧ the kitchen became a dining room when a two-story kitchen and playroom addition was built ❧ finally, after all three kids got through college, we added a private bath with two well-lit walk-in closets ❧ now bill can tell on a sunday morning whether the suit he pulls out is navy or black!

dogs and kids and lots of friends have snuggled in daybeds, curled up in window seats, and sipped lemonade on the front porch ❧ sooner or later, though, everyone seems drawn to the old brick fireplace in the kitchen (the brick came from the building where bill went to high school) where in three seasons of the year there is a log fire burning ❧ in the summer i line the hearth with big chunky candles ❧ spring, summer, fall, winter—the hearth seems to be the heart of this place ❧ and if that hearth could talk it would sing the anthem of our lives.

gloria gaither
*august 1999*

As the soul is the center of ourselves, this hearth has been the center of our home ❧ Like a great heart pulsating the rhythm of life, this hearth dances with the flames that warm and enliven the routine of our days ❧

As a

reflection of

the love that burned

within our hearts and

drew our two separate

lives to the warmth and

light of its fire, we

built this hearth

WHEN

NIGHTS WERE COLD

WE BUILT A FIRE, AND

YOU KEPT IT GOING

ALL THROUGH

THE NIGHT

In the morning, I would stir the embers and add kindling ❧ the sparks would ignite the wood, and the fire would blaze again ❧

By the time the coffee was made, the warmth of this fire would draw you to me, and together we would begin a new day.

At the
end of the day,
we would share
a simple meal
by this fire and
recount the day's
successes and
failures

$W$HEN

THE JOYS

OUTWEIGHED THE

DISAPPOINTMENTS,

WE CELEBRATED

*BY THIS FIRE* ❧

WHEN THE FAILURES

OUTWEIGHED THE

SUCCESSES, WE

HELD EACH

OTHER CLOSE

*BY THIS FIRE* ❧

e ENLARGED

THE BOUNDARIES OF OUR HOME

BY THIS FIRE ❧ WE DEVELOPED

NEW FRIENDSHIPS AND EXPLORED

NEW IDEAS. . . GAINED NEW

INSIGHTS AND WROTE NEW SONGS

❧ HOW WE LAUGHED BY THIS

FIRE! ❧ BY THIS FIRE WE

WARMED OUR BABIES AND GAZED

IN WONDER AT THE MIRACLE

OF A NEW LIFE WE HAD

TOGETHER CREATED AND

BROUGHT INTO THE WORLD ❧

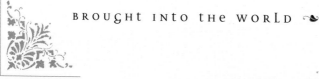

AS THEY GREW, WE ROCKED

OUR BABIES *BY THIS fire*

AND READ THEM STORIES,

TOLD THEM TALES, AND PASSED

ON OUR MEMORIES ❧

To this

hearth freshly

bathed, little

bodies were

carried, swaddled

in towels to be

dressed for

bed in long,

flannel

pajamas

By this fire many pairs of mittens and boots, countless wool caps and snow suits have been hung to dry after their owners have given a day to the snow kingdom

Beside *this fire* quarts of hot chocolate and gallons of coffee have been sipped over hours of happy conversation

**B**y this
fire promises have been
made, vows exchanged,
problems solved, and
mountainous obstacles
moved by prayer 🐦 by this
fire poetry has been created
and recited, and great ideas
have been discussed 🐦

$B$y

*this fire*

HOMEWORK HAS

BEEN DONE

$B$y
this fire we
have packed boxes
for college . . .

HEMMED WEDDING

DRESSES AND

ARRANGED BRIDAL

BOUQUETS. . .

AND DANCED WITH

EXCITEMENT AT THE

ANNOUNCEMENT

OF A NEW BABY

ON THE WAY . . .

$B$y

*this fire* we

have cut the red

raspberry cake

for dozens of

birthdays . . .

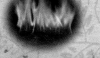

. . . planned fourth

of july picnics . . .

packed for

vacations . . .

AND STOOD WITH

RELATIVES, GIVING

THANKS FOR

THOSE THINGS

FOR WHICH WE'RE

MOST GRATEFUL

SINCE LAST WE

TOLD THE STORY

OF OUR PILGRIM

HERITAGE

We have celebrated the christmases of our lives by this fire

$W_e$ have made

chocolate and

fruitcakes,

. . . strung

popcorn

and cranberries;

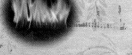

. . . made clay

ornaments . . .

and wrapped

dozens of

gifts

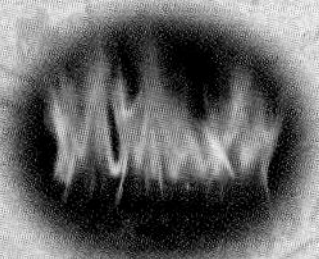

We

HAVE ARRANGED

THE NATIVITY WITH

CARE AND AWE . . .,

AND WE HAVE

TOLD THE

CHILDREN WHY . .

AGAIN AND AGAIN

We have

trimmed the tree with

treasured ornaments,

lit the star, and hung

the mistletoe by this

fire ❧ by this fire

we have bid farewell

to the old year

. . . and welcomed the

new ❧ We have begun

again, by this fire ❧

**O**VER

THE YEARS

AND *BY THIS FIRE*,

COMMUNITY HAS

FLOURISHED,

RELATIONSHIPS

HAVE DEEPENED,

INTIMACY HAS BEEN

RESTORED, AND

FRIENDSHIPS HAVE

BEGUN AND BEEN

RENEWED

By this

*fire*, tears of

remorse,

estrangement,

reconciliation,

celebration,

revelation,

and bereavement

have been shed

As the

seasons changed,

this mantle has

been decorated

with spring

flowers, summer

branches, and

birds,

fall leaves and

harvest bounty,

pine, holly,

bittersweet

and berries

Always,
THE MANTLE CLOCK

HAS MARKED THE

TIME BETWEEN

SUNDAYS WHEN THE

WINDING OF ITS

WORKS CELEBRATED

THE RITUAL OF THE

LORD'S DAY ❧

THIS FIRE

HAS LIT THE INNOCENT

faces of babies;

THE EXUBERANT faces OF CHILDREN;

THE HOPEFUL faces OF YOUTH;

THE WORRIED, RELIEVED, PONDEROUS,

REALISTIC faces OF PARENTS; THE

FURROWED, RESIGNED, WISE, AND

amused faces OF THE AGED

ike our

hearts, this fire holds

the memories, the secrets,

the dreams, and the

aspirations of

our home ❧

And when the clock on the mantel is still, and the hearth has cooled, and the house is empty, then things we've shared by this fire will have been branded on our very souls.

# The Love

we've shared *by this fire*

will burn forever ❧